Backyard Jungle
SAFARI
RED FOXES

Nicole Orr

PURPLE TOAD
PUBLISHING

Printing   1   2   3   4   5   6   7   8   9

BACKYARD JUNGLE SAFARI

Red Foxes
Gray Squirrels
Opossums
Raccoons

Publisher's Cataloging-in-Publication data
Orr, Nicole.
  Red foxes / written by Nicole Orr.
    p. cm.
Includes bibliographic references and index.
ISBN 9781624690983
1. Red fox—Juvenile literature.   2. Red fox—Vocalization. 3. Red fox—Behavior—Juvenile literature. 4.Red fox—Development—Juvenile literature. I. Series : Backyard jungle safari.
 QL737 2015
 599.775

Library of Congress Control Number: 2014945187

eBook ISBN: 9781624690990

ABOUT THE AUTHOR: Nicole Orr has been writing for ten years. In that time, she's participated in National Novel Writing Month eight times, written over 30 fictional novels for fun, and become a freelance transcriptionist. Since finishing this book, Orr has been eager to write zombie foxes into her next novel.

PUBLISHER'S NOTE: The information in this book has been researched in depth, and to the best of our knowledge is correct. Although every measure is taken to give an accurate account, Purple Toad Publishing makes no warranty of the accuracy of the information and is not liable for damages caused by inaccuracies.

BACKYARD JUNGLE
SAFARI
RED FOXES

RED FOXES

It is a cold winter night in the woods. Andy is camping in a cabin with his parents. He hears a wailing noise. He looks out the window. Is it a ghost? No! It is the cry of a red fox.

Red foxes are even hairier than they look! Not only do they have whiskers on their face, but they have them on their legs, too.

Look at a fox's eyes. Do they look more like a dog's or a cat's? If you guessed a cat's, you're right! Just like cats, foxes can see in the dark too.

A group of foxes is called a skulk. Don't confuse it with a skunk. Skunks are smellier!

BEING A FOX

The next morning, Andy walks outside. The ground is covered in animal prints. "Those are fox prints," his dad points out. "Did you hear that wail last night? It was a female fox, or a vixen. She is searching for a mate. The males, called dogs, fight over the vixen. The strongest dog wins."

What do human kids have in common with fox pups? They both like to wrestle and some like to climb trees!

"Do all foxes wail like that?" Andy asks.
"Foxes can make two dozen noises. A quick yap shows anger. A sharp bark warns of danger. Female foxes whine softy to their babies. This is called 'gekkering.' Andy's dad looks closely at his son. "Can you gekker, Andy?"
"No!" Andy laughs. "I'm not a fox. I'm a boy!"

They might look scary, but foxes are very friendly. They will follow a cat or dog around until they give up and become friends.

LEARNING TO HUNT

"Do foxes have big families?" Andy asks. "They have as many as a dozen babies at a time," says Andy's Dad. "The brown or gray pups are very small and could fit in your hand. Their ears and eyes are shut. When they open, the pups wrestle and play. They learn hunting skills from their father."

In many fairy tales, foxes are sneaky and very clever.

Andy's dad bends down and makes a snowball. He tosses it at Andy. Andy ducks. Andy throws one back. It hits his dad's arm. Splat! "A dog teaches his pups how to hunt," Andy's dad says. "They sit quietly next to a burrow until a mouse sticks its head out. They sneak up on their prey. They run! They pounce!"

Pups find it fun to chew on each other's ears and tails.

Male foxes aren't just called dogs. Sometimes they're called reynards. *Renard* is the French word for fox!

"Why don't the mice see them?" Andy asks.

"When foxes are grown, their fur is red. They blend in with leaves and bushes. They are very fast, too. They can run almost as fast as a car on the highway," Andy's dad smiles. "The dog dances, too."

"Why?" Andy frowns.

"He's showing off for rabbits. The rabbits come closer. They are curious and then they become dinner!"

Rabbits are one of the fox's favorite foods. If there are a lot of rabbits in a part of the woods, chances are there will be a lot of foxes too.

Foxes are born with blue eyes. As adults, their eyes turn brown.

The whiskers of foxes are very sensitive. They can even feel prey moving through the grass.

Andy looks around. "What do foxes eat?"

"They snack on birds, bugs, berries, and even worms!" Andy's dad laughs. "If the dog brings back more food than his family can eat, he buries it for later. To protect their land, they also pee on it. This is called scent marking."

Many human kids don't like to eat their veggies. Some foxes don't either! They eat mostly meats and fruits.

IN THE CITY OR FOREST?

"How do foxes stay warm?" asks Andy, pulling his hat down over his ears.

"Red foxes stay in dens, called earths. Some are made out of left over holes from other animals. Foxes might also dig their own. The vixen uses her tail or 'brush' as a blanket to keep her babies warm."

Andy smiles. He likes his thick sleeping bag better.

Most fox dens are made to face the sun. Why? Because this helps keep the pups warm.

"I wish foxes lived near us," says Andy. "Some do," his dad says. "In the city, they are called urban foxes. Your Mom and I wish they would go away! They eat out of our trash cans. They make a mess. They steal pet food. In the wild, foxes live only five or six years. In the city, there are more dangers. There are big cars. There are big dogs. There are big humans. These are all threats."

What does a fox's fur smell like? A little like a skunk. Foxes have two *scent glands.* These make a smell that scares off enemies.

27

A vixen uses her tongue for getting tough seeds out of her tail.

Foxes are a lot like cats. They like to eat mice, and they use their tongues to stay clean. But Foxes are not related to cats. They are part of the dog family.

At night, Andy crawls under the covers. He hears another ghostly wail. This time he doesn't go to the window. He knows—it is just the cry of a red fox.

What is one of the best ways to know what foxes eat? Look at their poo, also called *scat*.

FURTHER READING

Books

Geisel, Theodor. *Fox in Socks: Dr. Seuss's Book of Tongue Tanglers*. Random House Books for Young Readers: New York, 2011.

Gliori, Debi. *No Matter What*. Houghton Mifflin Harcourt Books for Young Readers: Boston, 2008.

Gliori, Debi. *Stormy Weather*. Walker Children's: London, 2009.

Spinelli, Eileen. *Miss Fox's Class Shapes Up*. Albert Whitman and Company: Morton Grove, IL, 2011.

Spinelli, Eileen. *Peace Week in Miss Fox's Class*. Albert Whitman and Company: Morton Grove, IL, 2009.

Works Consulted

Lantier, Patricia, and Judy Schuler. *The Wonder of Foxes*. Gareth Stevens Publishing: Milwaukee, 2001.

Leach, Michael. *Fox*. PowerKIDS Press: New York, 2009.

Lockwood, Sophie. *Foxes*. The Child's World: Mankato, MN, 2008.

McDonald, Mary Ann. *Foxes*. The Child's World: Mankato, MN, 2008.

Person, Stephen. *Arctic Fox*. Bearport Publishing, Inc.: New York, 2009.

Phillips, Dee. *Fox's Den*. Bearport Publishing, Inc.: New York, 2012.

"Red Foxes," *National Geographic A–Z*. Accessed: September 12, 2013. http://animals.nationalgeographic.com/animals/mammals/red-fox/?source=A-to-Z

On the Internet

Animals Time: Red Fox Facts for Kids, http://animalstime.com/red-fox-facts-kids-red-fox-habitat-diet/

Environmental Education for Kids (EEK): The Red Fox, http://dnr.wi.gov/eek/critter/mammal/redfox.htm

Switch Zoo: Red Fox, http://www.switcheroozoo.com/profiles/redfox.htm

INDEX